THIS JOURNAL BELONGS TO:

Jalila

A GIRL'S PRAYER JOURNAL
PB & J Prayers, Vol. 1

A *Girl's* PRAYER JOURNAL

PB & J *Prayers*

VOL. 1

Hi there!

Welcome to your new "PB & J" Prayer Journal. You are about to start a great adventure--of getting to know God better through prayer! But before you jump in, here are a few things to know before you start.

WHY USE A PRAYER JOURNAL?

If you hadn't eaten for a week, how would feel about a PB&J sandwich? I'll bet you'd be pretty excited about it, wouldnt you? Eating food fills up our stomachs and gives renewed energy for the day. It takes the hunger away so we can enjoy our life.

Just like your stomachs, your hearts can feel "hungry" too--you get hungry for God! You might notice yourself feeling worried, or crabby, or sad, or overwhelmed. Those are all signs that your heart is hungry: You need to fill up with God!

A lot of people just think of prayer as a chance to ask God for everything *they* want, and then they move on with their day. But that's like eating a bite of a sandwich, instead of enjoying the whole thing! It's not really enough to fill you up and give you the strength you need.

In addition to telling God the things you want, you can also use prayer to praise God and bless others. You can listen to God's Word and think about what *He* wants too.

> DON'T SETTLE FOR LITTLE "BITES" OF PRAYER. TAKE TIME TO EAT A WHOLE PRAYER "SANDWICH" AND HAVE A DEEPER CONVERSATION WITH GOD!

By adding these things to your prayers, you "fill up" your heart--with gratitude and trust and love. And this prayer journal can help you do that. So don't settle for little "bites" of prayer. Take time to eat a whole prayer "sandwich" and have a deeper conversation with God!

THANK-YOU FOR:

_____

_____

_____

_____

FORGIVE ME FOR:

_____

_____

_____

_____

People To Pray For

Help Me Show Love Today By:

_____

_____

On My Mind

Tell God about your worries and desires.

God, I give all my worries, fears, and desires to you. Please help me to trust you today.

B

READ "Be kind and compassionate to one another, forgiving each other, just as in Christ God forgave you."

- Ephesians 4:32

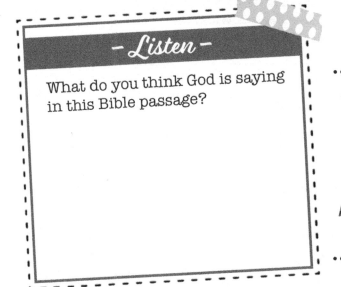

— Listen —

What do you think God is saying in this Bible passage?

PRAY

ASK GOD TO GIVE YOU A FORGIVING HEART THAT WILL STILL LOVE PEOPLE EVEN WHEN THEY'RE MEAN OR ANNOYING.

WONDER Is there anyone you feel angry with today? Who did something annoying or hurt your feelings?

_____

_____

_____

_____

THANK-YOU FOR:

_____

_____

_____

_____

FORGIVE ME FOR:

_____

_____

_____

_____

People To Pray For

Help Me Show Love Today By:

_____

_____

On My Mind

Tell God about your worries and desires.

God, I give all my worries, fears, and desires to you. Please help me to trust you today.

J

READ "You saw me before I was born. Every day of my life was recorded in your book. Every moment was laid out before a single day had passed."

- Psalm 139:16 (NLT)

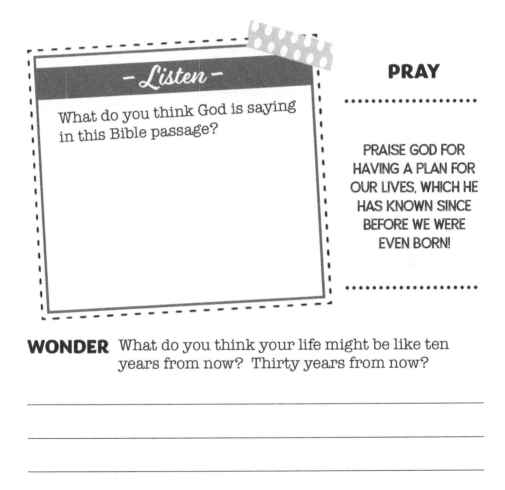

– Listen –

What do you think God is saying in this Bible passage?

PRAY

· · · · · · · · · · · · · · · · · ·

PRAISE GOD FOR HAVING A PLAN FOR OUR LIVES, WHICH HE HAS KNOWN SINCE BEFORE WE WERE EVEN BORN!

· · · · · · · · · · · · · · · · · ·

WONDER What do you think your life might be like ten years from now? Thirty years from now?

_____

_____

_____

_____

THANK-YOU FOR:

_____

_____

_____

_____

FORGIVE ME FOR:

_____

_____

_____

_____

People To Pray For

Help Me Show Love Today By:

_____

_____

On My Mind

Tell God about your worries and desires.

. . . .

God, I give all my worries, fears, and desires to you. Please help me to trust you today.

. . . .

READ "The Lord sustains them on their sickbed and restores them from their bed of illness."

- Psalm 41:3

- Listen -

What do you think God is saying in this Bible passage?

PRAY

. . . .

PRAY FOR A FRIEND OR FAMILY MEMBER WHO IS SICK. ASK GOD TO GIVE THEM COMFORT AND STRENGTH DURING THIS HARD TIME, AND TO HEAL THEM.

. . . .

WONDER Imagine meeting someone who's never been sick: How would you explain what it's like to be sick?

_____

_____

_____

_____

THANK-YOU FOR:

_____

_____

_____

_____

FORGIVE ME FOR:

_____

_____

_____

_____

People To Pray For

Help Me Show Love Today By:

_____

_____

On My Mind

Tell God about your worries and desires.

God, I give all my worries, fears, and desires to you. Please help me to trust you today.

B

— Join —

READ "Don't look out only for your own interests, but take an interest in others, too."

- Philippians 2:4 (NLT)

— Listen —

What do you think God is saying in this Bible passage?

PRAY

....

ASK GOD TO HELP
YOU PAY ATTENTION
TO THE NEEDS
OF OTHERS,
NOT JUST YOUR
OWN NEEDS.

....

WONDER When was the last time you let someone else go first? Or stopped to help someone out?

_____

_____

_____

_____

THANK-YOU FOR:

_____

_____

_____

_____

FORGIVE ME FOR:

_____

_____

_____

_____

People To Pray For

Help Me Show Love Today By:

_____

_____

On My Mind

Tell God about your worries and desires.

God, I give all my worries, fears, and desires to you. Please help me to trust you today.

– Praise –

READ "Therefore, I urge you, brothers and sisters, in view of God's mercy, to offer your bodies as a living sacrifice, holy and pleasing to God—this is your true and proper worship."

- Romans 12:1

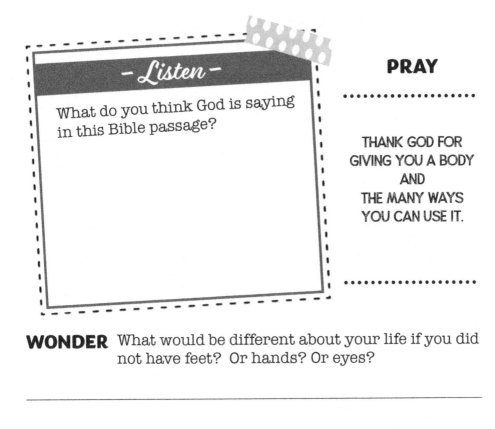

– Listen –

What do you think God is saying in this Bible passage?

PRAY

. . . .

THANK GOD FOR
GIVING YOU A BODY
AND
THE MANY WAYS
YOU CAN USE IT.

. . . .

WONDER What would be different about your life if you did not have feet? Or hands? Or eyes?

_____

_____

_____

_____

THANK-YOU FOR:

_____

_____

_____

_____

FORGIVE ME FOR:

_____

_____

_____

_____

On My Mind

Tell God about your worries and desires.

People To Pray For

God, I give all my worries, fears, and desires to you. Please help me to trust you today.

Help Me Show Love Today By:

_____

_____

READ "But love your enemies, do good to them, . . . Then your reward will be great, and you will be children of the Most High, because he is kind to the ungrateful and wicked. Be merciful, just as your Father is merciful."

- Luke 6:35-36

— Listen —

What do you think God is saying in this Bible passage?

PRAY

PRAY FOR THE PERSON WHO MAKES YOU THE MOST ANNOYED OR ANGRY RIGHT NOW. ASK GOD TO BLESS THEM, AND TO HELP YOU SHOW THEM LOVE.

WONDER What people are hard to get along with? Is there someone who often makes you feel annoyed or mad?

_____

_____

_____

_____

THANK-YOU FOR:

_____

_____
_____
_____
_____

FORGIVE ME FOR:

_____
_____
_____
_____

People To Pray For

Tell God about your worries and desires.

God, I give all my worries, fears, and desires to you. Please help me to trust you today.

Help Me Show Love Today By:

_____
_____

B

READ "Children, obey your parents in everything, for this pleases the Lord."

- Colossians 3:20

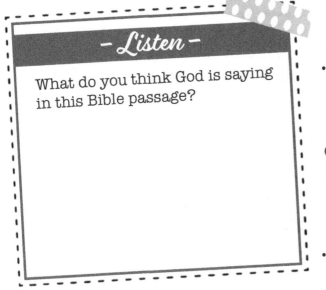

– Listen –

What do you think God is saying in this Bible passage?

PRAY

ASK GOD TO HELP YOU RESPECT AND OBEY YOUR PARENTS, EVEN WHEN YOU FEEL FRUSTRATED WITH THEM.

WONDER What are some things you appreciate about your parents? What is something that you *don't* like them to do?

THANK-YOU FOR:

_____

_____

_____

_____

_____

FORGIVE ME FOR:

_____

_____

_____

_____

_____

People To Pray For

Help Me Show Love Today By:

_____

_____

Tell God about your worries and desires.

God, I give all my worries, fears, and desires to you. Please help me to trust you today.

J

— Praise —

READ "Dear friends, let us love one another, for love comes from God. Everyone who loves has been born of God and knows God. Whoever does not love does not know God, because God is love. This is how God showed his love among us: He sent his one and only Son into the world that we might live through him." - 1 John 4:7-9

— Listen —

What do you think God is saying in this Bible passage?

PRAY

· · · · · · · · · · · · · · · · · · ·

PRAISE GOD FOR BEING A GOD OF PERFECT LOVE AND FOR SHOWING HIS LOVE BY SENDING JESUS TO GIVE US LIFE

· · · · · · · · · · · · · · · · · · ·

WONDER How would you describe love? How do you show love?

_____

_____

_____

_____

THANK-YOU FOR:

_____

_____

_____

_____

_____

FORGIVE ME FOR:

_____

_____

_____

_____

_____

People To Pray For

Help Me Show Love Today By:

_____

_____

On My Mind

Tell God about your worries and desires.

. . . .

God, I give all my worries, fears, and desires to you. Please help me to trust you today.

. . . .

READ "I pray that out of his glorious riches he may strengthen you with power through his Spirit in your inner being, so that Christ may dwell in your hearts through faith."

- Ephesians 3:16-17

— *Listen* —

What do you think God is saying in this Bible passage?

PRAY

. . . .

PRAY FOR YOUR NEIGHBORS. ASK GOD TO BLESS THEM AND MAKE THEM STRONG IN FAITH.

. . . .

WONDER What are three interesting things you know about the neighbors who live near you?

_____

_____

_____

_____

THANK-YOU FOR:

_____

_____

_____

_____

FORGIVE ME FOR:

_____

_____

_____

_____

People To Pray For

Help Me Show Love Today By:

_____

_____

On My Mind

Tell God about your worries and desires.

God, I give all my worries, fears, and desires to you. Please help me to trust you today.

B

Join

READ "Don't be selfish; don't try to impress others. Be humble, thinking of others as better than yourselves."

- Philippians 2:3 (NLT)

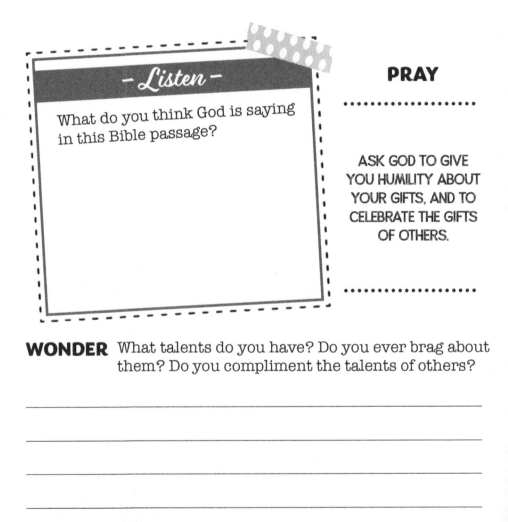

- Listen -

What do you think God is saying in this Bible passage?

PRAY

....

ASK GOD TO GIVE YOU HUMILITY ABOUT YOUR GIFTS, AND TO CELEBRATE THE GIFTS OF OTHERS.

....

WONDER What talents do you have? Do you ever brag about them? Do you compliment the talents of others?

_____

_____

_____

_____

THANK-YOU FOR:

_____

_____

_____

_____

_____

FORGIVE ME FOR:

_____

_____

_____

_____

People To Pray For

Help Me Show Love Today By:

_____

_____

On My Mind

Tell God about your worries and desires.

God, I give all my worries, fears, and desires to you. Please help me to trust you today.

Praise

READ "Because you are my help, I sing in the shadow of your wings."
- Psalm 63:7

"My help comes from the LORD, the Maker of heaven and earth."
- Psalm 121:2

– Listen –

What do you think God is saying in this Bible passage?

PRAY

· · · · · · · · · · · · · · · · · · · ·

SAY A PRAYER, OR SING A SONG OF PRAISE, TO THANK GOD FOR PROVIDING YOU WITH HELP WHEN YOU NEED IT.

· · · · · · · · · · · · · · · · · · · ·

WONDER What is one way that you received help from someone today?

_____

_____

_____

_____

THANK-YOU FOR:

(blank lines)

FORGIVE ME FOR:

(blank lines)

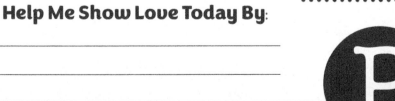

People To Pray For

Help Me Show Love Today By:

(blank lines)

On My Mind

Tell God about your worries and desires.

God, I give all my worries, fears, and desires to you. Please help me to trust you today.

READ "Carry each other's burdens, and in this way you will fulfill the law of Christ."

- Galatians 6:2

— *Listen* —

What do you think God is saying in this Bible passage?

PRAY

. . . .

PRAY FOR SOMEONE GOING THROUGH A HARD TIME: ASK GOD TO SEND THE HELP THEY NEED TO FACE THEIR DIFFICULT SITUATION.

. . . .

WONDER Is there a classmate/friend who is struggling with something hard right now? How could you show support?

_____

_____

_____

_____

THANK-YOU FOR:

_____
_____
_____
_____
_____

FORGIVE ME FOR:

_____
_____
_____
_____
_____

On My Mind

Tell God about your worries and desires.

People To Pray For

God, I give all my worries, fears, and desires to you. Please help me to trust you today.

Help Me Show Love Today By:

_____
_____

B

READ "Those who guard their mouths and their tongues keep themselves from calamity."

- Proverbs 21:23

"The wise listen to advice."

- Proverbs 12:15

— Listen —

What do you think God is saying in this Bible passage?

PRAY

. . . .

ASK GOD TO HELP YOU BE A GOOD LISTENER AND TO GAIN WISDOM FROM THE ADVICE OF OTHERS.

. . . .

WONDER What are some benefits you gain by listening? Who are some wise people you can listen to?

_____

_____

_____

_____

THANK-YOU FOR:

_____

_____

_____

_____

FORGIVE ME FOR:

_____

_____

_____

_____

People To Pray For

Help Me Show Love Today By:

_____

_____

On My Mind

Tell God about your worries and desires.

God, I give all my worries, fears, and desires to you. Please help me to trust you today.

READ "All Scripture is God-breathed and is useful for teaching, rebuking, correcting and training in righteousness."

- 2 Timothy 3:16

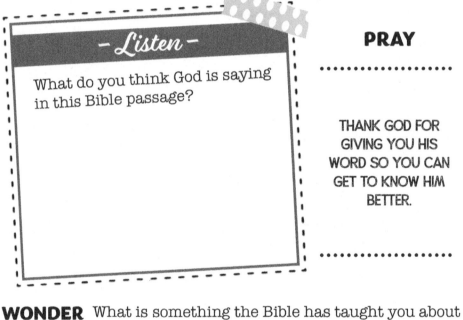

― Listen ―

What do you think God is saying in this Bible passage?

PRAY

THANK GOD FOR GIVING YOU HIS WORD SO YOU CAN GET TO KNOW HIM BETTER.

WONDER What is something the Bible has taught you about God? What has it taught you about people?

THANK-YOU FOR:

_____

_____

_____

_____

FORGIVE ME FOR:

_____

_____

_____

_____

People To Pray For

Help Me Show Love Today By:

_____

_____

On My Mind

Tell God about your worries and desires.

God, I give all my worries, fears, and desires to you. Please help me to trust you today.

Bless

READ "Even to your old age and gray hairs I am he, I am he who will sustain you. I have made you and I will carry you; I will sustain you and I will rescue you."

- Isaiah 46:4

- Listen -

What do you think God is saying in this Bible passage?

PRAY

PRAY FOR YOUR GRANDPARENTS AND ELDERLY FRIENDS. ASK GOD TO GIVE THEM STRENGTH AND ENERGY FOR EACH DAY.

WONDER What would be a good thing about being old? What would be a hard thing?

_____

_____

_____

_____

THANK-YOU FOR:

_____

_____

_____

_____

FORGIVE ME FOR:

_____

_____

_____

_____

On My Mind

Tell God about your worries and desires.

People To Pray For

God, I give all my worries, fears, and desires to you. Please help me to trust you today.

Help Me Show Love Today By:

_____

_____

B

READ "I pray that you may enjoy good health and that all may go well with you, even as your soul is getting along well."

- 3 John 1:2

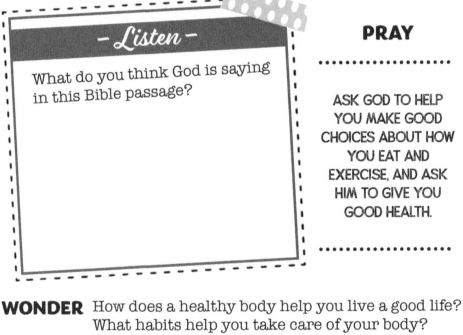

– Listen –

What do you think God is saying in this Bible passage?

PRAY

ASK GOD TO HELP YOU MAKE GOOD CHOICES ABOUT HOW YOU EAT AND EXERCISE, AND ASK HIM TO GIVE YOU GOOD HEALTH.

WONDER How does a healthy body help you live a good life? What habits help you take care of your body?

THANK-YOU FOR:

_____

_____

_____

_____

_____

FORGIVE ME FOR:

_____

_____

_____

_____

On My Mind

Tell God about your worries and desires.

People To Pray For

God, I give all my worries, fears, and desires to you. Please help me to trust you today.

Help Me Show Love Today By:

_____

_____

J

READ "The Lᴏʀᴅ will keep you from all harm—he will watch over your life; the Lᴏʀᴅ will watch over your coming and going both now and forevermore."

- Psalm 121:7-8

– *Listen* –

What do you think God is saying in this Bible passage?

PRAY

· ·

THANK GOD FOR KEEPING YOU SAFE DURING ALL THE TIME YOU'VE SPENT TRAVELING.

· ·

WONDER How many times have you gotten in a vehicle or walked outside this week? Where did you go?

_____

_____

_____

_____

THANK-YOU FOR:

_____

_____

_____

_____

FORGIVE ME FOR:

_____

_____

_____

_____

On My Mind

Tell God about your worries and desires.

People To Pray For

• • • • • • • • • • • • • • • • • • •

God, I give all my worries, fears, and desires to you. Please help me to trust you today.

• • • • • • • • • • • • • • • • • • •

Help Me Show Love Today By:

_____

_____

Bless

READ "Listen, my son, to your father's instruction and do not forsake your mother's teaching."

- Proverbs 1:8

– Listen –

What do you think God is saying in this Bible passage?

PRAY

PRAY FOR YOUR PARENTS. ASK GOD TO HELP THEM MAKE WISE CHOICES, AND TO HELP YOU RESPECT THEM AND LISTEN TO THEIR INSTRUCTION.

WONDER If you could make one new family rule, what would it be and why?

_____

_____

_____

_____

THANK-YOU FOR:

_____

_____

_____

_____

FORGIVE ME FOR:

_____

_____

_____

_____

People To Pray For

On My Mind

Tell God about your worries and desires.

God, I give all my worries, fears, and desires to you. Please help me to trust you today.

Help Me Show Love Today By:

_____

_____

B

READ "Therefore encourage one another and build each other up."
- 1 Thessalonians 5:11

"Let us consider how we may spur one another on toward love and good deeds."
- Hebrews 10:24

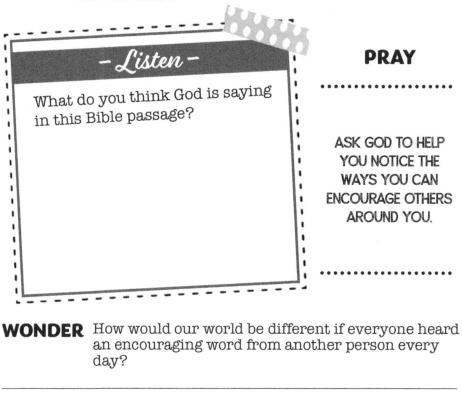

— Listen —

What do you think God is saying in this Bible passage?

PRAY

ASK GOD TO HELP YOU NOTICE THE WAYS YOU CAN ENCOURAGE OTHERS AROUND YOU.

WONDER How would our world be different if everyone heard an encouraging word from another person every day?

_____

_____

_____

_____

THANK-YOU FOR:

_____

_____

_____

_____

FORGIVE ME FOR:

_____

_____

_____

_____

People To Pray For

Help Me Show Love Today By:

_____

_____

On My Mind

Tell God about your worries and desires.

God, I give all my worries, fears, and desires to you. Please help me to trust you today.

J

Praise

READ "When you have eaten and are satisfied, praise the LORD your God for the good land he has given you."

- Deuteronomy 8:10

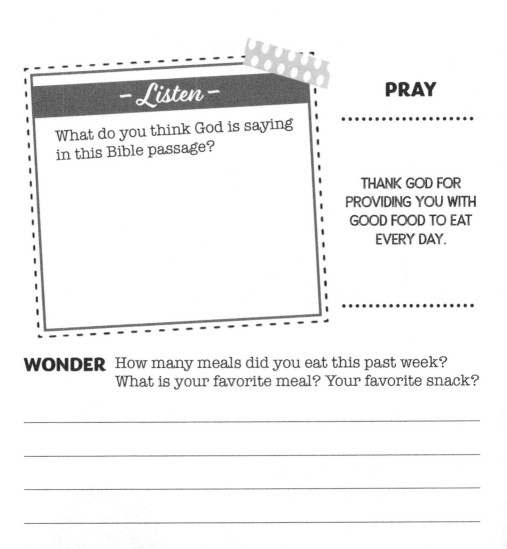

Listen

What do you think God is saying in this Bible passage?

PRAY

THANK GOD FOR
PROVIDING YOU WITH
GOOD FOOD TO EAT
EVERY DAY.

WONDER How many meals did you eat this past week? What is your favorite meal? Your favorite snack?

_____

_____

_____

_____

THANK-YOU FOR:

_____

_____

_____

_____

FORGIVE ME FOR:

_____

_____

_____

_____

People To Pray For

Help Me Show Love Today By:

_____

_____

On My Mind

Tell God about your worries and desires.

God, I give all my worries, fears, and desires to you. Please help me to trust you today.

READ "He will judge between the nations and will settle disputes for many peoples. They will beat their swords into plowshares and their spears into pruning hooks. Nation will not take up sword against nation,nor will they train for war anymore."

- Isaiah 2:4

– Listen –

What do you think God is saying in this Bible passage?

PRAY

• • • • • • • • • • • • • • • • • •

PRAY FOR FAMILIES THAT LIVE IN WAR-TORN COUNTRIES. PRAY FOR AN END TO THE CONFLICTS SO PEACE AND SAFETY CAN BE RESTORED.

• • • • • • • • • • • • • • • • • •

WONDER What would be different about your life if you lived in a country where there is war?

_____

_____

_____

_____

THANK-YOU FOR:

_____

_____

_____

_____

FORGIVE ME FOR:

_____

_____

_____

_____

On My Mind

Tell God about your worries and desires.

People To Pray For

God, I give all my worries, fears, and desires to you. Please help me to trust you today.

Help Me Show Love Today By:

_____

_____

B

READ "Do not conform to the pattern of this world, but be transformed by the renewing of your mind. Then you will be able to test and approve what God's will is—his good, pleasing and perfect will."

- Romans 12:2

- Listen -

What do you think God is saying in this Bible passage?

PRAY

ASK GOD TO HELP YOU STAY STRONG IN WHAT YOU BELIEVE, AND NOT TO CAVE IN TO PRESSURE TO ACT LIKE OTHERS.

WONDER Do you ever feel weird because of what you believe? Do you ever feel tempted to act like everyone else--even when you know it's not right?

_____

_____

_____

_____

THANK-YOU FOR:

_____

_____

_____

_____

FORGIVE ME FOR:

_____

_____

_____

_____

People To Pray For

Help Me Show Love Today By:

_____

_____

On My Mind

Tell God about your worries and desires.

God, I give all my worries, fears, and desires to you. Please help me to trust you today.

— Bless —

READ "Defend the weak and the fatherless; uphold the cause of the poor and the oppressed."

- Psalm 82:3

"Blessed are the peacemakers."

- Matthew 5:9

— Listen —

What do you think God is saying in this Bible passage?

PRAY

PRAY FOR POLICE AND FIRE FIGHTERS IN YOUR CITY. ASK GOD TO PROTECT THEM AND TO HELP THEM BRING JUSTICE IN YOUR COMMUNITY.

WONDER What do you think police or firefighters like about their jobs? What would they *not* like?

_____

_____

_____

_____

THANK-YOU FOR:

_____

_____

_____

_____

FORGIVE ME FOR:

_____

_____

_____

_____

People To Pray For

Help Me Show Love Today By:

_____

_____

Tell God about your worries and desires.

God, I give all my worries, fears, and desires to you. Please help me to trust you today.

B

READ "Bear with each other and forgive one another if any of you has a grievance against someone. Forgive as the Lord forgave you. And over all these virtues put on love, which binds them all together in perfect unity."

- Colossians 3:13-14

– Listen –

What do you think God is saying in this Bible passage?

PRAY

· · · · · · · · · · · · · · · · ·

ASK GOD TO GIVE YOU A SPIRIT OF UNITY WITH YOUR PARENTS AND SIBLINGS, SO YOUR FAMILY CAN BE A PICTURE OF GOD'S PEACE AND LOVE.

· · · · · · · · · · · · · · · · ·

WONDER What is the last thing you had a fight about in your family? What do you tend to argue about most?

_____

_____

_____

_____

THANK-YOU FOR:

_____

_____

_____

_____

FORGIVE ME FOR:

_____

_____

_____

_____

People To Pray For

Help Me Show Love Today By:

_____

_____

On My Mind

Tell God about your worries and desires.

God, I give all my worries, fears, and desires to you. Please help me to trust you today.

J

READ "He is the Rock, his works are perfect, and all his ways are just. A faithful God who does no wrong, upright and just is he."

- Deuteronomy 32:4

— *Listen* —

What do you think God is saying in this Bible passage?

PRAY

PRAISE GOD TODAY
FOR BEING
ALL-POWERFUL
AND FAIR.
THANK HIM FOR
ALWAYS USING HIS
POWER FOR GOOD.

WONDER Can you think of a leader from history who used his power to hurt people?

_____

_____

_____

_____

THANK-YOU FOR:

_____

_____

_____

_____

_____

FORGIVE ME FOR:

_____

_____

_____

_____

_____

People To Pray For

Help Me Show Love Today By:

_____

_____

On My Mind

Tell God about your worries and desires.

God, I give all my worries, fears, and desires to you. Please help me to trust you today.

Bless

READ "The foreigner residing among you must be treated as your native-born. Love them as yourself, for you were foreigners in Egypt. I am the LORD your God."

- Leviticus 19:34

- Listen -

What do you think God is saying in this Bible passage?

PRAY

....

PRAY FOR REFUGEES WHO ARE FORCED TO LEAVE THEIR COUNTRIES AND START LIFE OVER IN A NEW COUNTRY.

....

WONDER If your family moved to a different country, what are some things you would have to learn in order to live there?

_____

_____

_____

_____

THANK-YOU FOR:

_____

_____

_____

_____

FORGIVE ME FOR:

_____

_____

_____

_____

People To Pray For

Help Me Show Love Today By:

_____

_____

On My Mind

Tell God about your worries and desires.

God, I give all my worries, fears, and desires to you. Please help me to trust you today.

B

READ "No one has ever seen God; but if we love one another, God lives in us and his love is made complete in us."

- 1 John 4:12

- Listen -

What do you think God is saying in this Bible passage?

PRAY

....

ASK GOD TO SHOW
YOU HOW YOU CAN
SHARE HIS LOVE WITH
OTHERS.

....

WONDER What is something loving that was done for you this week? What is something loving that you could do for someone else this week?

_____

_____

_____

_____

THANK-YOU FOR:

_____

_____

_____

_____

_____

FORGIVE ME FOR:

_____

_____

_____

_____

_____

People To Pray For

Help Me Show Love Today By:

_____

_____

On My Mind

Tell God about your worries and desires.

God, I give all my worries, fears, and desires to you. Please help me to trust you today.

J

Praise

READ "For all have sinned and fall short of the glory of God, and all are justified freely by his grace through the redemption that came by Christ Jesus."

- Romans 3:23-24

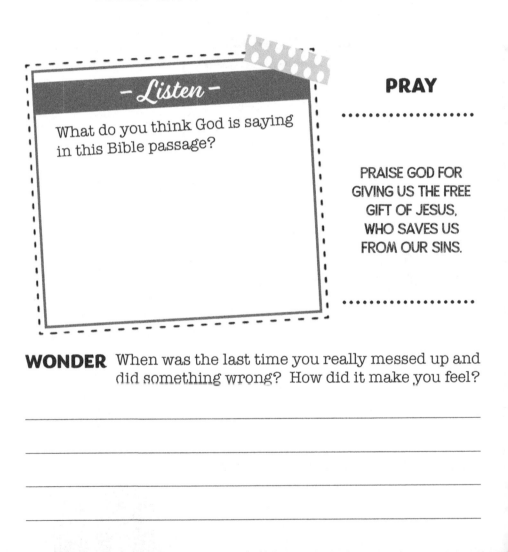

- Listen -

What do you think God is saying in this Bible passage?

PRAY

· · · · · · · · · · · · · · · · · · · ·

PRAISE GOD FOR GIVING US THE FREE GIFT OF JESUS, WHO SAVES US FROM OUR SINS.

· · · · · · · · · · · · · · · · · · · ·

WONDER When was the last time you really messed up and did something wrong? How did it make you feel?

_____

_____

_____

_____

THANK-YOU FOR:

_____

_____

_____

_____

FORGIVE ME FOR:

_____

_____

_____

_____

People To Pray For

Help Me Show Love Today By:

_____

_____

On My Mind

Tell God about your worries and desires.

God, I give all my worries, fears, and desires to you. Please help me to trust you today.

READ "There will always be poor people in the land. Therefore I command you to be openhanded toward your fellow Israelites who are poor and needy in your land."

- Deuteronomy 15:11

- Listen -

What do you think God is saying in this Bible passage?

PRAY

PRAY FOR PEOPLE WHO DON'T HAVE ENOUGH FOOD. ASK GOD TO HELP THEM FIND THE RESOURCES THEY NEED.

WONDER How do you act when you are hungry? What does your body feel like when it needs food?

THANK-YOU FOR:

_____

_____

_____

_____

FORGIVE ME FOR:

_____

_____

_____

_____

People To Pray For

Help Me Show Love Today By:

_____

_____

On My Mind

Tell God about your worries and desires.

God, I give all my worries, fears, and desires to you. Please help me to trust you today.

B

READ "My grace is sufficient for you, for my power is made perfect in weakness."

- 2 Corinthians 12:9

"I can do all this through him who gives me strength."

- Philippians 4:13

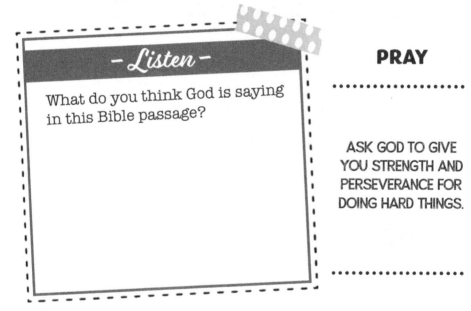

— Listen —

What do you think God is saying in this Bible passage?

PRAY

· · · · · · · · · · · · · · · · ·

ASK GOD TO GIVE YOU STRENGTH AND PERSEVERANCE FOR DOING HARD THINGS.

· · · · · · · · · · · · · · · · ·

WONDER What is something you have to do right now that feels very hard for you to do? (ex. school project, a hard person to deal with, a temptation or hard task.)

_____

_____

_____

_____

THANK-YOU FOR:

_____

_____

_____

_____

FORGIVE ME FOR:

_____

_____

_____

_____

People To Pray For

Help Me Show Love Today By:

_____

_____

Tell God about your worries and desires.

God, I give all my worries, fears, and desires to you. Please help me to trust you today.

J

– Praise –

READ "Be strong and courageous. Do not be afraid or terrified because of them, for the Lᴏʀᴅ your God goes with you; he will never leave you nor forsake you."

- Deuteronomy 31:6

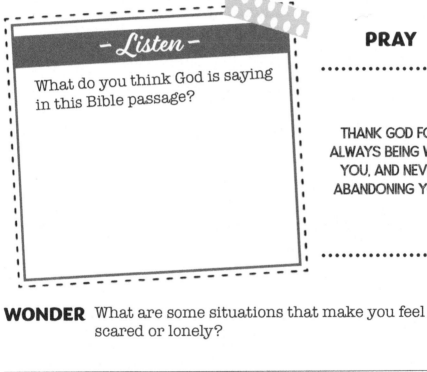

– Listen –

What do you think God is saying in this Bible passage?

PRAY

· ·

THANK GOD FOR ALWAYS BEING WITH YOU, AND NEVER ABANDONING YOU.

· ·

WONDER What are some situations that make you feel scared or lonely?

THANK-YOU FOR:

_____

_____

_____

_____

FORGIVE ME FOR:

_____

_____

_____

_____

On My Mind

Tell God about your worries and desires.

People To Pray For

God, I give all my worries, fears, and desires to you. Please help me to trust you today.

Help Me Show Love Today By:

_____

_____

READ "Humble yourselves, therefore, under God's mighty hand, that he may lift you up in due time. Cast all your anxiety on him because he cares for you."

- 1 Peter 5:6-7

- Listen -

What do you think God is saying in this Bible passage?

PRAY

PRAY FOR SOMEONE WHO IS LOOKING FOR A JOB. ASK GOD TO GIVE THEM PATIENCE AND TO TRUST THAT GOD WILL PROVIDE WHAT THEY NEED.

WONDER What kind of job do you think you might enjoy working someday?

_____

_____

_____

_____

THANK-YOU FOR:

_____

_____

_____

_____

FORGIVE ME FOR:

_____

_____

_____

_____

On My Mind

Tell God about your worries and desires.

People To Pray For

God, I give all my worries, fears, and desires to you. Please help me to trust you today.

Help Me Show Love Today By:

_____

_____

B

READ "Set a guard over my mouth, LORD; keep watch over the door of my lips."
- Psalm 141:3

"Speak up for those who cannot speak for themselves; ensure justice for those being crushed."
- Proverbs 31:8 (NLT)

- Listen -

What do you think God is saying in this Bible passage?

PRAY

· · · · · · · · · · · · · · · · · ·

ASK GOD TO HELP YOU LISTEN AT THE RIGHT TIMES, AND TO SPEAK UP AT THE RIGHT TIMES.

· · · · · · · · · · · · · · · · · ·

WONDER What is harder for you: To be quiet at times when you should be listening? Or to speak up at times when others are doing wrong?

_____

_____

_____

_____

THANK-YOU FOR:

_____

_____

_____

_____

FORGIVE ME FOR:

_____

_____

_____

_____

*People
To Pray For*

God, I give all my
worries, fears, and
desires to you.
Please help me to
trust you today.

Help Me Show Love Today By:

_____

_____

J

READ "Jesus looked at them and said, 'With man this is impossible, but with God all things are possible.' "

- Matthew 19:26

— Listen —

What do you think God is saying in this Bible passage?

PRAY

PRAISE GOD
THAT HE CAN DO
THINGS THAT LOOK
IMPOSSIBLE TO US.

WONDER Can you list four miraculous events that happened in the Bible?

_____

_____

_____

_____

THANK-YOU FOR:

_____

_____

_____

_____

FORGIVE ME FOR:

_____

_____

_____

_____

People To Pray For

Help Me Show Love Today By:

_____

_____

God, I give all my worries, fears, and desires to you. Please help me to trust you today.

READ "I urge, then, first of all, that petitions, prayers, intercession and thanksgiving be made for all people—for kings and all those in authority, that we may live peaceful and quiet lives in all godliness and holiness."

- 1 Timothy 2:1-2

— *Listen* —

What do you think God is saying in this Bible passage?

PRAY

. . . .

PRAY FOR WORLD LEADERS. ASK GOD TO BRING GOOD PEOPLE TO POWER WHO WILL FIGHT INJUSTICE & PROMOTE PEACE.

. . . .

WONDER What are the signs of a good leader? What are the signs of a bad leader?

_____

_____

_____

_____

THANK-YOU FOR:

_____

_____

_____

_____

FORGIVE ME FOR:

_____

_____

_____

_____

People To Pray For

On My Mind

Tell God about your worries and desires.

God, I give all my worries, fears, and desires to you. Please help me to trust you today.

Help Me Show Love Today By:

_____

_____

B

READ "Watch and pray so that you will not fall into temptation. The spirit is willing, but the flesh is weak."

- Matthew 26:41

"Submit yourselves, then, to God. Resist the devil, and he will flee from you."

- James 4:7

- Listen -

What do you think God is saying in this Bible passage?

PRAY

· · · · · · · · · · · · · · · · ·

ASK GOD TO HELP YOU NOTICE WHEN YOU'RE BEING TEMPTED AND TO BE STRONG ENOUGH TO DO THE RIGHT THING.

· · · · · · · · · · · · · · · · ·

WONDER What are some wrong things that you have felt tempted to do in the past?

_____

_____

_____

_____

THANK-YOU FOR:

_____
_____
_____
_____

FORGIVE ME FOR:

_____
_____
_____
_____

People To Pray For

Help Me Show Love Today By:

_____
_____

On My Mind

Tell God about your worries and desires.

God, I give all my worries, fears, and desires to you. Please help me to trust you today.

J

Praise

READ "God saved you by his grace when you believed. And you can't take credit for this; it is a gift from God."

- Ephesians 2:8 (NLT)

– Listen –

What do you think God is saying in this Bible passage?

PRAY

. . . .

THANK GOD THAT HE DOESN'T MAKE US EARN HIS LOVE, BUT GIVES IT TO US A GIFT.

. . . .

WONDER How do people earn good grades, or money? How does it feel to know you don't have to earn God's love?

_____

_____

_____

_____

THANK-YOU FOR:

_____

_____

_____

_____

FORGIVE ME FOR:

_____

_____

_____

_____

People To Pray For

Help Me Show Love Today By:

_____

_____

On My Mind

Tell God about your worries and desires.

· · · · · · · · · · · · · · · · · · · ·

God, I give all my worries, fears, and desires to you. Please help me to trust you today.

· · · · · · · · · · · · · · · · · · · ·

READ "So do not fear, for I am with you; do not be dismayed, for I am your God.
I will strengthen you and help you; I will uphold you with my righteous right hand."

- Isaiah 41:10

- Listen -

What do you think God is saying in this Bible passage?

PRAY

PRAY FOR DOCTORS AND NURSES AT YOUR LOCAL HOSPITAL AND THE PEOPLE WHO NEED THEIR HELP. PRAY THAT GOD WILL GUIDE THEIR HANDS TO BRING HEALING.

WONDER Have you ever visited a hospital? Have you ever been a patient there? What was it like?

THANK-YOU FOR:

_____

_____

_____

_____

_____

FORGIVE ME FOR:

_____

_____

_____

_____

_____

People To Pray For

Help Me Show Love Today By:

_____

_____

On My Mind

Tell God about your worries and desires.

God, I give all my worries, fears, and desires to you. Please help me to trust you today.

B

READ "Whoever is kind to the poor lends to the LORD, and he will reward them for what they have done."

- Proverbs 19:17

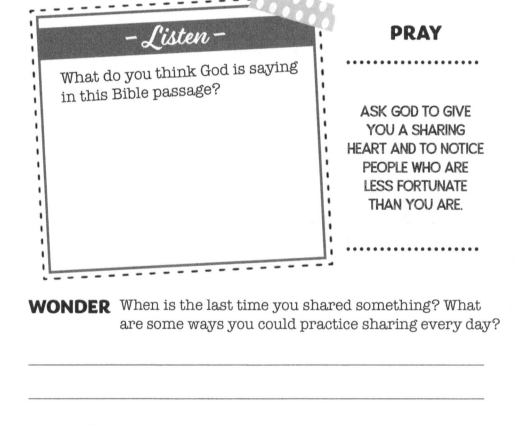

— Listen —

What do you think God is saying in this Bible passage?

PRAY

· · · · · · · · · · · · · · · · · · · ·

ASK GOD TO GIVE YOU A SHARING HEART AND TO NOTICE PEOPLE WHO ARE LESS FORTUNATE THAN YOU ARE.

· · · · · · · · · · · · · · · · · · · ·

WONDER When is the last time you shared something? What are some ways you could practice sharing every day?

_____

_____

_____

_____

THANK-YOU FOR:

_____

_____

_____

_____

FORGIVE ME FOR:

_____

_____

_____

_____

People To Pray For

Help Me Show Love Today By:

_____

_____

On My Mind

Tell God about your worries and desires.

God, I give all my worries, fears, and desires to you. Please help me to trust you today.

J

READ "But you, O Lᴏʀᴅ, will sit on your throne forever. Your fame will endure to every generation."

- Psalm 102:12 (NLT)

"Look, God is greater than we can understand. His years cannot be counted."

- Job 36:26 (NLT)

− *Listen* −

What do you think God is saying in this Bible passage?

PRAY

. . . .

PRAISE GOD FOR BEING EVERLASTING-- FOR BEING AT WORK THROUGH ALL OF HISTORY.

. . . .

WONDER Can you name a person who lived 100 years ago? 500 years ago? 5,000 years ago?

_____

_____

_____

_____

THANK-YOU FOR:

_____

_____

_____

_____

FORGIVE ME FOR:

_____

_____

_____

_____

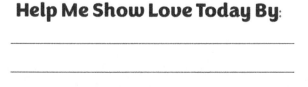

People To Pray For

Help Me Show Love Today By:

_____

_____

Tell God about your worries and desires.

· · · · · · · · · · · · · · · · · · ·

God, I give all my worries, fears, and desires to you. Please help me to trust you today.

· · · · · · · · · · · · · · · · · · ·

Bless

READ "Anyone who loves their brother and sister lives in the light, and there is nothing in them to make them stumble."

- 1 John 2:10

- Listen -

What do you think God is saying in this Bible passage?

PRAY

PRAY FOR YOUR BROTHERS AND SISTERS. PRAY THAT GOD WOULD HELP YOU LOVE EACH OTHER AND BE A SUPPORTIVE TEAM TO KEEP EACH OTHER FROM STUMBLING.

WONDER What is one thing you like about each of your siblings? (If you don't have siblings, think of a friend!)

_____

_____

_____

_____

THANK-YOU FOR:

_____
_____
_____
_____
_____

FORGIVE ME FOR:

_____
_____
_____
_____

People To Pray For

Help Me Show Love Today By:

_____
_____

B

— Join —

READ "Therefore each of you must put off falsehood and speak truthfully to your neighbor, for we are all members of one body."

- Ephesians 4:25

— Listen —

What do you think God is saying in this Bible passage?

PRAY

· · · · · · · · · · · · · · · · · · ·

ASK GOD TO HELP YOU SPEAK THE TRUTH AT ALL TIMES SO THAT YOU DO NOT HURT PEOPLE WITH YOUR LIES.

· · · · · · · · · · · · · · · · · · ·

WONDER How do you feel when someone tells you a lie?

_____

_____

_____

_____

THANK-YOU FOR:

_____

_____

_____

_____

FORGIVE ME FOR:

_____

_____

_____

_____

People To Pray For

Help Me Show Love Today By:

_____

_____

On My Mind

Tell God about your worries and desires.

· · · · · · · · · · · · · · · · · ·

God, I give all my worries, fears, and desires to you. Please help me to trust you today.

· · · · · · · · · · · · · · · · · ·

– Praise –

READ "Every good and perfect gift is from above, coming down from the Father of the heavenly lights, who does not change like shifting shadows."

- James 1:17

– Listen –

What do you think God is saying in this Bible passage?

PRAY

....

SAY A PRAYER THANKING GOD FOR GIVING YOU THIS WONDERFUL GIFT/KINDNESS.

....

WONDER What is a gift you recently received? Is there an act of kindness someone did for you today?

_____

_____

_____

_____

THANK-YOU FOR:

_____
_____
_____
_____
_____

FORGIVE ME FOR:

_____
_____
_____
_____

People To Pray For

Help Me Show Love Today By:
_____
_____

On My Mind

Tell God about your worries and desires.

God, I give all my worries, fears, and desires to you. Please help me to trust you today.

P

Bless

READ "Land that drinks in the rain often falling on it and that produces a crop useful to those for whom it is farmed receives the blessing of God."

- Hebrews 6:7

– Listen –

What do you think God is saying in this Bible passage?

PRAY

PRAY FOR THE FARMERS WHO LIVE NEAR YOU. ASK GOD TO BLESS THEM WITH HEALTHY ANIMALS AND A GOOD HARVEST.

WONDER If you could work on a farm for a day, what jobs would you like to do? What jobs would you *not* like to do?

_____

_____

_____

_____

THANK-YOU FOR:

_____

_____

_____

_____

FORGIVE ME FOR:

_____

_____

_____

_____

People To Pray For

Help Me Show Love Today By:

_____

_____

God, I give all my worries, fears, and desires to you. Please help me to trust you today.

B

READ "Don't use foul or abusive language. Let everything you say be good and helpful, so that your words will be an encouragement to those who hear them."

- Ephesians 4:29 (NLT)

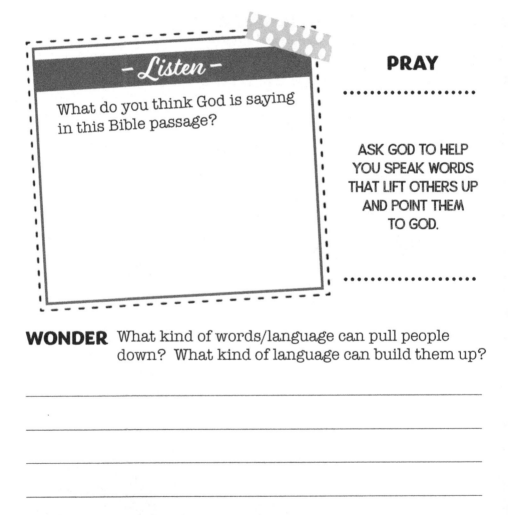

– Listen –

What do you think God is saying in this Bible passage?

PRAY

. . . .

ASK GOD TO HELP YOU SPEAK WORDS THAT LIFT OTHERS UP AND POINT THEM TO GOD.

. . . .

WONDER What kind of words/language can pull people down? What kind of language can build them up?

_____

_____

_____

_____

THANK-YOU FOR:

_____
_____
_____
_____

FORGIVE ME FOR:

_____
_____
_____
_____

People To Pray For

On My Mind

Tell God about your worries and desires.

God, I give all my worries, fears, and desires to you. Please help me to trust you today.

Help Me Show Love Today By:

_____
_____

J

YOUR THOUGHTS MATTER!

● ● ● ● ● ● ● ● ● ● ● ● ● ● ● ● ● ●

Did you enjoy using this prayer journal? Would you like to help other kids enjoy it too?

This is a small family-run business and we could use **your help** in spreading the word about our PB & J Journals! We would love to have you leave a great review wherever you purchased this journal. (Just be sure to ask your parents first.)

And I'd be happy to hear from you too! You can reach me at:

amy@morelikegrace.com

HOW ABOUT SOME FREEBIES?

Ask a Parent to Help You Explore These **Free** Printable Resources For Your Whole Family!

- Nature Scripture Scavenger Hunt
- Choose Your Own Adventure Bible-Reading Plan
- Scripture Prayer Cards for Kids
- Lunchbox Notes
- "Least of These" Family Prayer Chain
- *And many, many more!*

AVAILABLE AT **WWW.MORELIKEGRACE.COM**

(LOOK UNDER "FREE PRINTABLES")

MORE GREAT WAYS TO
GROW IN YOUR FAITH!

PB & J Prayer Journals

Fruit of the Spirit Bible Study

Made in the USA
Middletown, DE
11 November 2019